MENDING HOLES
IN THE SOUL WITH
GOD'S LOVE

Rosemarie McHenry

A wholly owned subsidiary of **TBN**

Mending Holes in the Soul with God's Love

Trilogy Christian Publishers A Wholly Owned Subsidary of Trinity Broadcasting Network

2442 Michelle Drive Tustin, CA 92780

Cover design by: Trilogy

For information about special discounts for bulk purchases, please contact Trilogy Christian Publishing.

Trilogy Disclaimer: The views and content expressed in this book are those of the author and may not necessarily reflect the views and doctrine of Trilogy Christian Publishing or the Trinity Broadcasting Network.

Manufactured in the United States of America

10 9 8 7 6 5 4 3 2 1

Library of Congress Cataloging-in-Publication Data is available.

ISBN: 978-1-68556-266-3

E-ISBN: 978-1-68556-267-0

DEDICATION

This book is dedicated to Frank Visentin. Without his continued encouragement and support, this book would have never happened.

Thank you, dear.

CONTENTS

PREFACE

Hello, my name is Rosemarie McHenry, and I am the author of this book. It took nine years to produce this work, and it represents my history from Victim to Victor. I've also put three surprises in the book. They were Visions from God, and He wanted me to write them. (Visions—don't let that word scare you away. In Acts 2:17, the Bible says, "And it shall be in the last days, saith God, I will pour out My Spirit upon all flesh, and your sons and your daughters shall prophesy, and your young men shall see visions, and your old men shall dream dreams.") I have helped a lot of hurting people with these visions, along with the information from my past. I feel there is something in this book for everyone.

Who would have ever thought that a child as damaged as I was would be able to produce a book to help others? Not all of my siblings went through what I went through, but the ones who did suffered through a childhood no one should have had to go through. I have poured out my heart and soul for all to see. I have finally let *all the secrets* come out into the light. Are you willing to come and take a journey with me? I promise you this journey leads back to wholeness.

There is a verse in the Bible in Genesis 50:20 that says, "You intended to harm me, but God intended it for

1

good to accomplish what is now being done, the saving of many lives." And you might have questions like I did. One of my biggest questions was: God, how could You let this happen to a three-year-old child? To my surprise, God answered these issues completely in the book.

One thing I want to assure you of is that it's okay to be angry at God. He knows your thoughts anyway, so you might as well just be honest since that anger generates the questions deep in your soul. God has absorbed an enormous amount of anger from me, and He loved me all the way through it. If you follow His path all the way to the end, He clears up all the questions. He cleared up my questions, but not in the way I thought He would.

I suffered extensive abuse as a child and clear through my teen years and beyond. Then, I married a man that I thought I would feel safe with, and he turned out not to be such a safe person. So, I went from an abusive childhood into an abusive marriage. That's because abusive treatment was what I was used to, and it was comfortable for me.

I found the Lord when I was eighteen. I wasn't looking for Him, honestly, but He was looking for me. I was standing by a pool and looking to heaven. I cried out and said, "God, if You are real, I have to know NOW!" A light came down from the sky and was positioned right in front of me. I felt a warmth and love radiating from the light. I knew it was Him! I stood there, knees shaking, and finally ran through the light, and a friend caught me and said, "I know what you went through." I said, "How could you possibly know?" She said, "Because your face is shining!" For the next two years, I don't think my feet touched the ground that whole time!

After suffering all this abuse, to finally experience true love for the first time, it was *overwhelming*. I have to say that God gave me two years of absolute love before He started training me to be one of His people. I say training because, as we know, the honeymoon doesn't last forever. I went from having His constant presence anytime I wanted it to experiencing His absence.

He began teaching me to live a life by faith and, to do that, He would stop talking to me for a period of time. There were times I would get so desperate to hear His voice and feel that close, loving relationship I used to have. Sometimes, I was sure that He had left me altogether. But He always came back and let me know that He was there the whole time but withheld His presence while He taught me to walk with Him by faith.

Have you ever read the book *Hinds Feet on High Places* by Hannah Hurnard? If you have not, I highly recommend it. It is an allegory of a young girl abused by her family who agrees to let the Lord train her for the Master's use. My path was quite similar to hers.

After walking with Jesus for fifty years, I can tell you He has changed my life. From the start, He began dealing with all the destruction in my life, and then, as a potter to a wheel, He started molding me and making me into something I never thought I could be. I am so different from when I first found the Lord. Not just the outward changes but inwardly, I have His presence and I seek to please Him, not out of duty, but because He is the love of my life. When God began dealing with all the wreckage in my life, I wished I had had a friend I could share things with.

Section One

MY JOURNEY

Having come from an abusive childhood, I have a lot of experience dealing with loss. The biggest loss, by far, was my childhood, and it took literally years of counseling to find that out. I am not going to dig through all those childhood traumatic details—I will spare you that. Suffice to say, my three sisters and I were raped, tortured, and prostituted by our own mother throughout our childhood to a dentist who had nine foster sons who made dirty home movies of us all, and this happened to me from the age of three to eleven. The foster boys were victims as well because if they did not perform as they were told, the dentist took a strap to them until they did.

At the age of eighteen, I was thrown out of the only home I had known. I began working, and through a very strange course of events, I found God. I have to say, when I found God, I discovered a warm, gentle love. I had never known love before that. My life had been so painful, and yet meeting God was such a warm, wonderful moment! And through another strange course of events, I also found His family (all the people who love God as well). And when I found God's family, I realized I was a part of that family because we all had the same Father. And for several years, I got lost in that family, and my childhood seemed to fade away into the background without making a sound.

I began, however, to realize that my "birth" family was different from these Christian families, who seemed so close and loving, and I began to notice small things like the hugging, the proper correction of bad behaviors, and most importantly, I noticed that no one ever got hurt. If the child did something wrong, the parents corrected him or her without calling the child names and without severe beatings.

I began observing them, almost like someone doing a research paper. Several of these families, over a period of years, let me live with them, and I became "family" with them. That allowed me to view their family from the "inside" and really watch and learn from them. I figured they could put on a show for a while, but when living with them, the show wouldn't last too long! But once there, I saw all the little "loving" things they did to and for each other, and it felt so foreign to me. I had never seen those behaviors before.

Being a part of this church put me with people who

were different from my past. They were nice to me, and they taught me how to enter into a relationship with God that I had never had before. I have to say that God became a "real" Father to me, and His people became closer to me than any brother or sisters in my birth family.

After a period of time, I thought it was time to start a family of my own. I began looking for Mr. Right, and that was a real project. The problem is, I didn't know how to have a relationship with someone. I mean, I saw it done in the families I lived with, but I soon realized that seeing it happen and actually doing it were two entirely different things!

But I found a man, and I will call him X for right now. He was kind and giving, and he seemed to know what love was. Of course, that is a statement coming from a person who was only guessing she knew what love was, since I didn't actually know what it was myself. He was a deacon in the church, so that made me at least feel safe. I decided to give it a try. We kind of did the dating thing, and I was kind of glad that the dating scene was over because I didn't know how to do it anyway. After only six weeks together, we were married.

He expected me to know how to be a wife, and I expected him to know how to be a husband since I was his second wife. I figured he must know something! However, I soon realized that this was a man who hadn't been married "successfully."

After a year and a half being married, it wasn't really working out well. So, we thought bringing children into the mix would help and had two children two years apart, even though I wasn't sure I even wanted them. It was just what I assumed was "expected" of the wife. I remember giving birth and holding this little blob, thinking: *And what am I supposed to do with this?* I called my mother to tell her she was a grandmother, and her exact words were, "Well, don't think you are bringing that d*** brat home for me to raise!" I was so shocked that I just hung up. I looked at the blob and said to myself, "Well, you are my family now."

And right from the start, the marriage wasn't going too well. After adding two children to the mix, I found it was harder than the other families had made it look, and when my marriage began falling apart, I wasn't sure how to stop it. Actually, if the truth be known, I wasn't sure if I even wanted to stop it.

I had a sad, sad life. And at this point in my life, I was kind of angry with God at how my life had turned out, as if it was all His fault. I guess you could say I didn't really know who to blame, so God was just there and present to accept the blame.

I could not accept responsibility for the failure of the marriage, even though I lacked the life skills to be married. When the marriage became violent, it seemed normal to me for a long time. But seeing successful marriages all around me became confusing when looking at my own. "Why do I have to suffer like this? My friends aren't suffering through their marriages." I could not answer my *own* questions. So, there I remained for twenty years in my own tailor-made hell. The marriage, however, ended with me divorcing him. I gave him everything: the million-dollar business we grew from scratch, a paid-for house, and numerous vehicles. All I took were my two kids— my oldest daughter, I will call her #1, and my youngest daughter, I will call her #2, and they were now almost as badly damaged as I was.

#1 decided at the age of fourteen she wasn't going to live with us anymore. She sat down with us and said, "You've been good parents up until now, but life is to be lived, and I'm going to start living it, so don't be offended!" I remember being confused by that statement. How does she think we have been good parents? Who has she measured us against to determine that? I thought I would lose my mind when she left home. I would comb the streets looking for her every night and didn't find her for months.

She became a dancer, living with anyone who would allow her to be there. She was always in trouble with the law, and they would always bring her back to our house after she got into trouble. They actually thought she lived there!

Every time she went to court, I had to go too. I would

tell the judge, "You just don't know her. She is a good kid, she went to Christian school, she was raised by me, and I know she is a good kid." The judge would let me take her home and said, "When you are sick of this nonsense, I will deal with it." It took another six months to get sick of it before I wrote a sixteen-page letter to the judge telling him, "I give up; you were right. And if you have any other parents as stupid as me, give them my name, and I will have a little chat with them" (he sent two sets of parents to me).

HOW I BEGAN HELPING OTHERS

#1 ended up in a level 8 program at a girl's home (semi-lockdown facility) five hours away. I drove from Palm Beach County north to Brevard County with bags of candy, sat on the picnic table eating the candy, talking to all the girls (except my own, who sat clear across the one-acre yard on a different picnic table). At first, it was just light chatter, but after a few weeks, they started telling me why they were there. Most of them had been abused by a parent, grandparent, uncle, neighbor, or friend. I sat and listened quietly to their stories, one by one, as they let their pain spill out. Each one said, "You have no idea how bad it was in my house, with this person, etc." I tried to tell them that the Bible says you need to forgive, but they could not hear that. They were in too much pain. So, I just listened for weeks! Then, when they ran out of tears, they said, "We don't know anything about you. Tell us about your life." "Oh, you don't want to hear that," I said. They literally forced it out of me. I had never told my pain to children before and wasn't sure if I should. I kept trying to avoid it. One day, one of the girls had gone home on furlough and came back abused all over again. She started to cry and tell us what had happened. I tried to comfort her, but she kept saying, "You have no idea what I have been through!"

I finally started talking to them about my childhood. Jaws dropped, tears dried up, and they just listened as I poured out my pain to them. But I didn't stop there; I kept on telling them the story of how I got through it. After all, that is the most important part. No one wants to live in pain; we all want to get past the pain and have a good life. I told them how I felt as they did, "Hell will freeze over before I forgive my mother!" But after I found the Lord, I came to realize that if I didn't forgive her, Jesus wouldn't forgive me. That seemed a bit unfair, and they all agreed. But I told them the prayer I prayed for twelve years: "God, I know Your Word says I *must* forgive, and I can mouth the words, but You see my heart, and You know my words would be a lie. You know, in my heart, I have *no* forgiveness for her. I can't even muster it up! So what do I do? I can't fake it because You would know anyway!"

Deep inside, I heard these words, "Then, ask me for forgiveness for your mother."

14

What a novel idea, "you have not because you ask not." So, I added on to my prayer these words: "Lord, if You want me to forgive my mother, then You are going to have to give me forgiveness *for* her because I have *none*! So, I give You permission to put forgiveness *in* me *for* her! And if You don't, I know it is because You can't even forgive her!"

So, every day I prayed that. Twelve long years I prayed that. I was sure Jesus couldn't even forgive her until one day I said, "Lord, I forgive my mother," and I stopped. The forgiveness happened, and I knew it was there, right inside of me. That voice deep inside me spoke again, "Now, call her and give it to her."

I got mad and said to God, "You want me to call her and let her off the hook? Why should she get a *pass* on something this horrific done to a small child?" It took three more years for me to be willing to call her and give her the forgiveness that I felt in my heart for her.

I called her and told her, "I remember *every single little thing you did to me, e-v-e-r-y-t-h-i-n-g*! But Jesus gave me forgiveness for you, and now I am calling to give it to you. In the name of Jesus, I forgive you."

There was silence on the phone. Defining silence. Then all at once, she spoke, "You're a *liar*! I did not do those things to you," and she slammed the phone down in my ear.

I sat there, stunned by what my own mother had said, till I began to realize that I felt like a thousand pounds fell off my back! *I was finally free!!!!* Joy was restored to me, and I was happy. I could not believe it.

All the girls sat there saying, "That would never happen to me! I can never forgive!"

I explained that forgiveness is not for them, it is for us. Most of them kept repeating that hell will freeze over before that happens to them. I said, "Right now, you are living in the hell of your emotions. Once you forgive, you are set free from hell, and that is exciting." I continued to explain that this doesn't mean you let that person continue the bad behavior. You may even need to prosecute them for the damage done to you, but you can do that and still forgive.

That is a hard concept to grasp, and it took about a month for that to settle in with them.

The girls went over to my daughter and said, "Wow, your mom is sooooooo cool!" #1 daughter popped up and said in a snotty angry voice, "You just don't *know* her!"

The next time I went there, the staff came to me and said, "What are you telling those girls?" I thought I was in trouble. They continued, "They are blossoming!" They told me that they had a conference room inside the building and asked if I could move in there with the girls. "We can then listen to you as you talk to them and see what you are doing that is helping these girls so much! You would be training us!" That went on for another couple of months, and eventually, #1 daughter came in and joined us. As new kids entered the program, they would cry their hearts out and then say, "You just don't know what I have been through." The other girls just popped up and said, "Oh, yes, she does, she really does!" By the time my daughter left that program, all these kids were well on their way to healing.

Section Two

MISSING PIECES

My mother just ignored all her children, and they seemed to make it through each year. I never had a relationship with my mother, my four sisters, or my only brother. We grew up like a family of strangers. When I gave birth to my firstborn, as I said before, I sat there holding it and crying, thinking, *Okay, now I have what everyone else has—just what am I supposed to do with it?* I had no clue what to do with a baby. That was kind of how my marriage went too. I never saw my mother and father hug or kiss, so how would I know to do that? They argued, they screamed, and as kids, we always seemed to fall right in the middle of it all!

Relationships were a puzzle. After going through a marriage, raising two children, and having just a few friends, certain, shall we say, deficiencies began to surface. I felt like everyone was one step ahead of me, and I felt like I was different from everyone else, somewhat unique! I was not sure where I fit in or if I fit in at all. I wasn't stupid—I had two years of college and a nursing degree behind my name. I knew how to care for people and be kind but never experienced it myself.

So, I began to do a little research about relationships. Why not? I knew how to do a research paper, so I watched my friends closely. I asked them questions about their relationship with their husband, their kids, and their grandparents, which looking back, they probably thought odd. Every piece of information was carefully recorded in my "relationships" journal or carefully logged into my memory for possible use later on. Can you imagine? Not knowing how to have a relationship with anyone? But then again—I'm getting ahead of myself. Let me back up a bit.

But what I didn't realize was this was only part of the healing. You see, it is not just what was done to you that needs healing; it's also about what *wasn't* done to you that needs to be mended. They are the "missing pieces" that need to be put back.

NIGHTMARES

I didn't remember my childhood until I hit thirty-six years old. I recall friends in elementary school saying they remember doing this or that with Mom or Dad when they were five years old, and I would jump right in their face and scream, "You are a liar! You don't remember when you were five years old! No one does!" They would scream at me, "Yes, I do!" and I would sock them dead in the face for being a liar! I got in more trouble doing that! Then in junior high, the same thing would happen, but by this time, the kids were too big to sock in the nose, so I just had to swallow it while rolling my eyes and calling them a liar under my breath!

Nevertheless, at age thirty-six, I began having a

nightmare of a child being attacked in bed at night. The attacker was faceless, and all I remember is waking up feeling so dirty and ashamed. After about a month of this nightmare happening, I went to sleep one night, and when the attacker appeared, the face was that of my brother. I woke up screaming and terrified. After that, violent nightmares of little children having awful things done to them played like a movie in my head. These nightmares began to roll in like a flood!

When I awoke, I could only remember the nightmare for a brief period of time, and then it left, leaving me feeling dirty and ashamed all over again. I decided to start writing down these nightmares. The funny thing is, when I began writing them down, I would read them a couple of hours later and could have sworn it was all someone else's vile thoughts, except for the fact that it was in my own handwriting.

This was when I sought help from a local minister. He listened to me read him the stories in my journal about these nightmares and, as kindly as he could, told me that he didn't think it was a nightmare. "I think it is a memory," he said. I told him that my parents were good people and could never do anything like that to me. The preacher encouraged me to continue writing my nightmares down. Soon after that session, other nightmares, more violent, came like a flood.

I was sent all the way to Colorado for Christian

counseling. After filling out a two-day detailed questionnaire about my childhood, they were sure it was childhood trauma. And after numerous sessions and reading my journal of dreams, the counselors silently determined the abuse was at my mother's own hands. As they worked with me, the nightmares came faster and more frequently. Faces began appearing in the nightmare, and I saw myself, then my brother's face appeared, and then my mother's. I recorded these nightmares as though my life depended on it because I now saw a glimpse of what the minister back in Florida had told me. They are dreams of *my* own past!

The counseling was going well until they began talking about forgiveness. I left the counseling facility in a rage, never to return, because they were pushing the "forgiveness" issue. I told them, "Hell would freeze over before I would forgive my mother for all the abuse and my dad for not protecting me from her!"

They told me that if I did not forgive her, I could not expect forgiveness. And I am not talking about the kind of forgiveness where someone hurts you, then they say they are sorry, and you utter those words, "I forgive you." I am talking about the kind of forgiveness given to someone who didn't admit what they did, didn't ask for your forgiveness, probably does not even feel like they need forgiveness from you, and for all intent and purposes, doesn't even deserve it. I think it is easy to forgive someone who is remorseful and asks for your forgiveness. What is really difficult is offering forgiveness to someone who doesn't deserve it.

During the past, when I could not deal with the turbulent issues in me, and I viewed God more as an enemy at this point in my life, I began going down a road I had never traveled. I began drinking.

My life went downhill quickly, and alcohol became my new best friend. It gave me a "life" at first, but then it became my master and took "life" from me. I think alcoholism is referred to as the "rapacious creditor" who takes life from you as if you owe it everything! I drank all the time, unable to control it, unable to stop it, and unable to be without it.

It got so bad that I decided to end my misery. I acquired four-quart bottles of my "poison of choice." I drank the first, then the next, and somewhere between the time I removed the cap from the 3rd bottle and the end of the bottle, I hit the floor. I laid there two and a half days on a hard tile floor. When I came to, even my hair hurt! Immediately I thought, *I could have died there!* I heard a voice in my head say, "And what makes you think you didn't! You took the gift of life I gave you and tried to piss it away!" Hearing these words, I knew it was God. I looked around as if to see if anyone could have heard what I just heard. I felt guilty, ashamed, and scared. I got into the shower, threw away all my clothes soiled by this incident, and made a decision.

I decided I would try something I had learned about a while back while on a job, where someone told me about AA.

So off I went to my first meeting. I found the people somewhat scary, but they welcomed me in with open arms. And after listening to them for a couple of days, I began to realize something. I finally found a lot of people *just like me*. As I got more involved, I found that these were people *exactly* like me. People full of the pain in their lives and full of defects, a lot of them had similarities to my childhood, but with slightly different details.

It was here that I found my higher power—the God of *my* understanding—and as I worked the steps, I became closer and closer with God again. My sponsor became like a mother figure to me, and the other men and women in there became my brothers and sisters. I had a family once again. As I continued to work the steps, I came to the step where you deal with "defects" and learned that all you can do with them is ask God to deal with them. If you seek Him, He will begin filling the holes as you do the work.

My defects, which I choose to call the "holes in my soul," were most likely the vital qualities or skills I should have learned as a child, or in school, or with family and friends, but never did. Or maybe I did possess these qualities or skills at one time but lost them due to adverse things happening in my life.

I was unclear how and why these holes appeared, and what's more, I didn't even know what disappeared from my life, creating the hole. And what's more, I didn't realize that a defect took the place of whatever it was that disappeared. Some of these qualities or skills that I am talking about are:

Quality/Skill	Possible defect that took its place
Joy	Anger/hate
Safety	Fear
Trust	Betrayal
Loving words	Criticism/sarcasm
Comfort	Torment
Truth	Lying
Pleasure	Pain
Secure	Abandonment
Peace	Stress
Friendship/companionship	Mental/physical solitude

I was now ten years clean and had completed the 12 steps. The problem is, my trust really wasn't there. How can you give everything over to God when you don't trust Him? Trust had been removed a long time ago. Something had to change!

I met a lot of people who wanted to talk about their past, and since they confided in me, I could tell them about myself. I then begin to help them work through their issues. It is helpful that I went through the twelve steps, which helped me to deal with my past and finally put it to bed. I am no longer a *victim* of my past! But not being a victim was only the beginning.

After working the steps (and let me assure you, it was hard work!) I was finally free of my past. And for a period of time, that was wonderful! But something began to appear. I came to realize that anger was settling in, and upon closer examination of this phenomenon, I realized that I was noticing all the "loss" experienced in my lifetime. You may say, "What exactly is loss?" I came to realize after about a year that what I am missing are all the things I was supposed to have learned or picked up during my lifetime but didn't or couldn't.

An example is *trust*. When you have been made to do things that you somehow knew were bad or unlawful but were forced to do them anyway by someone who was supposed to protect you. It creates a contradiction in your being. Hence, you began burying the shame of "forced" actions.

From that point on, it is difficult, if not impossible, to trust someone—especially someone you are supposed to trust, like a spouse or a pastor or even God. Now the cycle starts. The sad part is that you don't know you are *in a* cycle. To you, it is just normal life.

I began to notice families around me, successful families. They had lives that seemed to work. For me, I always thought everyone was just one step ahead of me, knew a little more than me, caught on one second faster, or was wise enough to have figured it out before I did. It was like I was swimming upstream!

This is typical for those of us who are full of holes. We are missing vital pieces of information that a lot of other people have. But how do we acquire those missing pieces? And since you never had what was missing, how do you know it is missing, and how do you find it?

I began to see areas in my life where I came up short. I am a smart businesswoman, able to run almost any software on the market and type 100 WPM. The deficiencies were not in my abilities; they were in my character.

The holes were gaping and painful. And Lord knows I tried filling them with everything I could think of. Sex, food, liquor, drugs, you name it! A lot of people try to fill it with porn, gambling, affairs, etc. But it is all the same—a substitute for the missing quality or attribute in our lives.

Section Three

SELF-DISCOVERY

Things eluded me, such as why can't I trust this certain person? Why am I afraid? Why can't I love? And what is love, after all? Can you see it? Feel it? What color is it? Or is it just that I am unlovable? Other people have it, feel it, can shake it off, "why can't I?" Mostly, these questions surrounded relationship issues in the beginning. I was not successful at them; neither did I care if I was successful at them. I just wondered WHY.

These questions haunted me about *relationships*. I began to write them down in a journal as questions to myself:

- What do I think love is?

- What do others think love is? (I asked other people or observed them.)

- What does God say love is? (I used my Bible for this one.)

- What makes a successful relationship (friendships, romantic, spiritual)?

- What is it about a relationship that makes me fearful?

- Why do I want to be romantically involved?

- What am I looking for in a relationship?

- What do I think a potential mate is looking for in a relationship?

- How do I feel about myself?

- How do others feel about me?

- How do I feel about others?

These were just some of the questions I asked myself. Every few days, I added to my answers, and I began to formulate theories about relationships. I tried some of them out. Some met with success, and others did not. I noted both the successes and the failures in my journal and kept doing research. And trust me when I say this research brought on even *more* questions I had to ask myself, such as questions about other issues, like *morals* or *feelings*. These brought on more and more questions, which revealed more and more deficiencies.

I became overwhelmed by how much I didn't know! It was as though I was peering through a magnifying glass to my very soul. *I felt cheated.* I had been right all these years. People knew things that I didn't know. These were things parents taught them. These were things that they learned in life experiences as they grew up under two loving parents. I didn't get that growing up in an unnatural habitat like my childhood home.

A very close friend taught me a skill. Take a problem, and go down one level by saying, "What caused this problem?" I wrote that down and then went down another level and another, asking, "What caused this feeling?" And as I kept taking it down level by level, I hit the "core" defect. After hitting the core, I thought I could see a way to fix it.

An example is: I was very critical. I took it down a level by asking, "Why am I so critical?" or "What happened that made me be critical?" Then, "What caused that feeling?" "When did this happen?" "Did I do this, or was it done to me, or in other words, what was my part in it?" That answer may be nothing as it might have been something that was done to you that caused this defect. When I got to the core, I realized what was missing.

Incomplete people can be resilient, and if you are one of them, you will have to want to give up that *very comfortable spot* of being a *victim*.

You have to look at your problems and say to yourself, "What was *my* part in all of this?" If you were abused like me, you think, "Hey, all of this was done *to* me—I had no part!" That thought is true, but as the victim, you have a part *now*, and that should be your focus.

But as you move on through life, you may or may not realize that the damage has been done *to you*! Now, how do you go about fixing it? That is how the healing *begins*. Look at *your* side of the street, not the other person's. What did *you* do, not what *they* did.

My First Vision from God

I was in the hospital getting tests done when I had a dream. I felt it was quite inspired. It came so effortlessly, and upon awakening, I was so taken back by it that I wrote it down. I also drew the example I saw in my dream. The dream played out like a motion picture playing in my head, it was so vivid, and it just seemed to pour out of me as I wrote it because all our holes are different.

This is what I wrote:

We are all damaged: by life, parents, friends, spouses, other so-called religious people, just to name a few. The point is, we all have holes in us. Some more than others, but we all have them. If you look at Diagram A, you will see what I mean. I purposely made it small, so you could not read it.

Diagram A

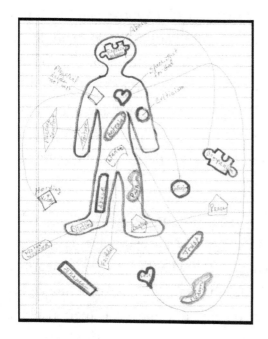

I want you to just focus on your initial reaction to the picture in Diagram A: a person standing there with pieces that have fallen out of him or her. We walk through life not even aware that those pieces are missing. I look at this dream like a puzzle with puzzle pieces missing. The overall picture is good, but the puzzle is still not complete.

During childhood, during our dealings with other people, etc., pieces are taken from us, especially if we were abused. However, the holes got there, we now have them to deal with. Then, as we go through life, we pick someone to marry, someone who we think can fill those holes left in us by our past; hence, we pick someone just like the abuser. Then, more holes happen, disappointments, and loss of things we really need, like love and trust. And the person we picked as a life partner has as many holes as we do, and they need their holes filled too. But you are busy trying to fill your holes; you are not too concerned with filling theirs. So that is when everything goes out of control. Everyone is trying to get their significant other to meet their needs without meeting their own. It is a vicious cycle.

As you begin life, you are, for the most part, whole. The only hole you have is that special place designated for God. We all have that. But what I have come to learn is that being a parent doesn't mean you do everything right. They do what their parents did and what their parents before them. They have a lot of "holes" passed down to them from generations before. And you will pass them down to your children unless you deal with them now. Diagram A shows the holes I saw in my vision while I was in the hospital.

So, as we go through our childhood, a lot of holes can appear. Those are some of the holes I saw at the time; however, you may have other holes that are completely different from mine because our lives went in different directions, and therefore the holes incurred are not the same. But in talking with other people since, I found that we do have a few holes "in common" with each other.

At first, you comfort those holes because they hurt, or

they make you feel "less than" or "inferior" to what you perceive other people to be.

For whatever reason, we let them go. We protect those holes in our soul because when we do, we feel better. For years, I poured alcohol into them, and that "numbed" the pain for a while. But as I became an alcoholic, the numbness wore off faster and faster, demanding that I fill them again and again.

The thing is, after years of suffering and pain, I realized God can fill all of those holes if you ask Him to. Of course, it will require that we maintain an active relationship with Him. He can give you the unconditional love you search for, and He can repair the trust issues and give you the joy you lost.

But we keep going back to "I want a man (or woman) to fill these holes in me," but we don't do the work to look at the holes and determine how to fix them. We just keep trying to get some man (or woman) to fill the holes for us, and that just isn't possible. And if you don't do the work, eventually, you may look to alcohol and drugs to fill them. Then, more issues are added to the mix. *If you don't do the work, you are doomed to repeat!*

That is why I say: do a little detective work. What are *your* needs that are going unmet, and what component do you feel is missing? What was *your* need? You had some holes you were trying to get another person to fill. What were they? Identify them so you don't keep this cycle happening over and over again!

Won't that be exciting? To share your *whole* life with another person who is *whole*? That is the part that is amazing. When you have done the work and cleared your pain, you know when you meet someone whether or not they are *whole*. It helps you make better choices. The second love of my life (we'll call him Adam) was completely different from my husband of twenty years, and I am completely different from when I was with my husband back then. Adam is kind, compassionate, considerate, and loves to make me happy. And I made him happy because I was not saddled with my issues. I am free to love and be loved. *What a wonderful feeling.*

My granddaughter has been damaged by both her drug and alcohol-addicted parents. The holes in her soul are visible, fresh, and painful. She is angry, hurt, does not trust anyone, and has recently turned to drugs to manage her life. I would love to talk to her about the holes and what is it she is looking to get filled. I would love to make her look at *herself*, not someone else or something else. It can be a long, tedious process, even arduous at times, but worth it.

I only say this because I have done it in my life. I have cleared away the wreckage of the past, so I can have a future, not as a victim but as a woman of integrity. I am no longer "needy." I am a *whole* person now. That is what the 12 steps have done for me.

That is not to say I am perfect. Far from it! But I no longer expect someone else to make me feel better about myself. I have gotten my self-image from seeing myself through God's eyes.

TWO FORCES PUSHING AT US

Body/physical world (what affects it?):

1. Abuse (physical, sexual, emotional, or verbal).

2. Deception.

3. Withholding affection.

4. Withholding love.

5. Withholding praise.

6. Withholding physical needs (a hug, food, clothing).

7. Distrust.

8. Incidents (life-changing, catastrophic) out of everyone's control.

9. Making fun of your appearance or being critical of it.

10. Name-calling.

11. Neglect (ignoring you).

12. Over-protection.

13. Keeping you from family, friends, division from siblings.

Core (we are in the image of God):

1. Love.

2. Peace.

3. Joy.

4. Forgiveness.

5. Physical needs.

6. Spiritual needs.

7. Emotional needs.

8. Desire.

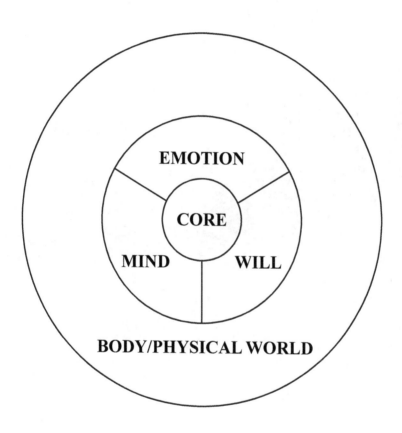

FORGIVENESS

This is a hard one. To tell you about this, I first must tell you that no one is perfect. When we refuse to forgive someone for an injustice, it is because we think they didn't do the right thing, that they weren't righteous. But are we always righteous? Do we always do the right thing?

As a child, I suffered torturous acts against me by my own mother, as did my sisters and my brother. I spent my first years of life being angry at my mother. And not just angry, I hated her. I hated what she was, what she did to me, what she made me do, and how she treated me. At age eighteen, I came to know Jesus. After all that hate festering for many years, I truly did not know what love was. But the day I met Jesus, I felt love for the first time in my life. And not just love, but unconditional love—which is unmerited, not deserved, and definitely not earned. It was so strong that at first, I didn't understand how He could give it. I was dirty and ashamed, and all I wanted to do was run from it. But His love grabbed hold of me and didn't let me run. And even though I didn't know this Jesus, I knew the second I felt the love that it belonged to Him. And when I got baptized, I felt so clean, like I was scrubbed with Comet cleanser and a scrub brush!

Now you might think that following that encounter, I forgave everyone who had ever wronged me, but that was not the case. His love came to me *unconditionally*. God never removes our free will to do what we want to do, think what we want to think, and say what we want to say. But does that mean I have the right to?

If you go to biblegateway.com, do a keyword search on the word "forgive," I believe it will shock you what you find.

Matthew 18, "The Parable of the Unmerciful Servant":

> *Then Peter came to Jesus and asked, "Lord, how many times shall I forgive my brother or sister who sins against me? Up to seven times?" Jesus answered, "I tell you, not seven times, but seventy-seven times. Therefore, the kingdom of heaven is like a king who wanted to settle accounts with his servants. As he began the settlement, a man who owed him ten thousand bags of gold was brought to him. Since he was not able to pay, the master ordered that he and his wife and his children and all that he had be sold to repay the debt. At this the servant fell on his knees before him.*

'Be patient with me,' he begged, 'and I will pay back everything.' The servant's master took pity on him, canceled the debt and let him go. But when that servant went out, he found one of his fellow servants who owed him a hundred silver coins. He grabbed him and began to choke him. 'Pay back what you owe me!' he demanded. His fellow servant fell to his knees and begged him, 'Be patient with me, and I will pay it back.' But he refused. Instead, he went off and had the man thrown into prison until he could pay the debt. When the other servants saw what had happened, they were outraged and went and told their master everything that had happened. Then the master called the servant in. 'You wicked servant,' he said, 'I canceled all that debt of yours because you begged me to. Shouldn't you have had mercy on your fellow servant just as I had on you?' In anger his master handed him over to the jailers to be tortured, until he should pay back all he owed. This is how my heavenly Father will treat each of you unless you forgive your brother or sister from your heart." Shouldest not thou also have had compassion on thy fellowservant, even as I had pity on thee? And his lord was wroth, and delivered him to the tormentors, till he should pay all that was due unto him. So likewise shall my heavenly Father do also unto you, if ye from your hearts forgive not every one his brother their trespasses.

Then, as if that is not clear enough, I find verses like this:

> *For if you forgive other people when they sin against you, your heavenly Father will also forgive you.* **Matthew 6:14**

> *But if you do not forgive others their sins, your Father will not forgive your sins.* **Matthew 6:15**

> *Then Peter came to Jesus and asked, "Lord, how many times shall I forgive my brother or sister who sins against me? Up to seven times?"* **Matthew 18:21**

> *"But I want you to know that the Son of Man has authority on earth to forgive sins." So he said to the man.* **Mark 2:10**

> *And when you stand praying, if you hold anything against anyone, forgive them, so that your Father in heaven may forgive you your sins.* **Mark 11:25**

> *If you forgive anyone's sins, their sins are forgiven; if you do not forgive them, they are not forgiven.* **John 20:23**

> *And when you stand praying, if you hold anything against anyone, forgive them, so that your Father in heaven may forgive you your sins.* **Mark 11:25**

So, this was my dilemma: I hated my mother, and rightly so. She did vile things to me as a child. And she didn't deserve forgiveness, so why was this Jesus insisting that I give it?

I grew up hating my mother, not trusting her, and not caring if she lived or died, and I didn't even know why. For *years*, my mind had blocked all of what happened to me as a child.

When the memories of my traumatic childhood began pouring out of my subconscious mind, they were so terrible, and I was terrified of them. It was a very dark time in my life, and alcohol became an intimate friend. I had to drink, as it was the only way I could close my eyes at night without seeing all the terror happening to a little girl.

Once I realized they were memories and not just nightmares, I had already had two children by then. They were six and four years old. What really stirred the anger up in me was when I began to realize that this was done to me from the age of three till I turned eleven years of age. Rage began to build. I looked into the sweet faces of my two daughters and thought, *what was wrong with me that my mom would do such awful things to me? What did I do wrong? Was I not smart enough?* My self-esteem took a dive because now I felt unlovable, undesirable, and stupid. I thought to myself, *I could never do that to my children. How is it that my mom felt she could do that to me, robbing me of my childhood?*

And I had every right to be angry. She hurt me and made me do things that I should never have had to do. But I have learned something about unforgiveness. To retain it is like drinking poison day after day, expecting the other person to die! And it is just that—poison! Trust me when I say I drank that poison for years just to spite her, and she didn't even know. She went on living her life while I cut myself off from her and suffered. "I'll teach her—I won't call her or talk to her ever again!" Trouble is, she could have cared less if I talked to her.

So, I began this journey. The more I read in the Bible about how I needed to forgive, the angrier I got. If I forgive her, she won't receive justice! I have to hold out and *make her pay*! But God was relentless. Everywhere I looked, forgiveness was being spoken about, taught, mentioned, etc. And inside my head, those verses were swirling and gnawing.

Finally, I began telling God, "I can mouth the words 'I forgive her,' but You know my heart, my thoughts, and my anger level. What do You want me to do? Just mouth the words? Even though You would know full well I don't mean them?"

That is when God spoke to me. "I Am." For a while, I just kept saying, "Am *what*?" But slowly, I began to realize that He is what I need. If I need forgiveness, I just need to ask my Jesus to put forgiveness into me because that was not a natural quality I possessed at that time.

It took me fifteen years, asking God every day to give me forgiveness *for* her. I remember I said the same thing I said every day for fourteen years, "Lord, I forgive her. You know that I don't have that to give her, so I ask You to deposit that in me *for* her." But the day finally came when I started saying this prayer for her, "Lord, I forgive her," and to my surprise, I actually forgave her.

That night, I was praying and thanking God for giving me the forgiveness in my heart for what she had done. And God spoke to me and said, "The forgiveness is for *her*. Give it to her." The next morning, I gathered my nerve and called her number. She answered. I began to speak, "Mom...I remember everything, *everything*! I remember what you did to me. I remember what you made me do, and I remember how it made me feel." And it came pouring out with tears. I told her that I forgave her.

She, however, was silent. When I finished pouring all of it out, I asked if she was still there and if she had something to say. She said, "You're a liar! I never did those things to you!" and she slammed down the phone.

I sat there silent, phone in hand, not knowing *how* to feel. But I soon began to realize there was *no more* anger or hate left in me for her. I just felt *free*! That verse came to mind, "If the Son therefore shall make you free, ye shall be free indeed" (John 8:36). And that was just how I felt.

And you might think that forgiving my mother was the end of it, but truly it was not. This freedom lasted for about eight months, and then I began to feel the anger swell again. But not for my mother; it was toward God. "How could You let her do this to an innocent child? Innocent children! Me and all my sisters!" I found no answers in the Bible except to realize that God never took away man's free will. My mother had a will to do this, and God could not take that free will away from her.

My feeling was, "Why could He not just burn the house down and kill us all? That would have been more humane!"

I was angry with God for about two to three years, and during that time, I was cussing like a truck driver! I couldn't stop it. The anger and rage had to get out. Finally, I got serious with God in one of my many nightly conversations with Him and said, "You know, I'm gonna let You slide on this issue for now. But if and when I get to heaven, face-to-face with you, I'm gonna *need* an answer." And I never again brought it up to God again.

Then began the process of forgiving myself. I didn't know for what; I just knew I had to do that. A couple of years into it, I realized that I needed to forgive myself for holding onto all of that from the past. I finally let it all go. My peace returned. That free feeling returned. I felt I could actually move on.

Something I have realized fifteen long years later from that parable quoted here about the king and the servant, I saw my mother as the servant who owed me a life. Something so huge! I was the king. The only thing is she never asked for forgiveness. I just gave it. She owed me, and she owed me *huge*. By forgiving her, that meant I would have to give up all claim to that expected payment. I had to give it to God, and He could do one of two things with this debt she owed. He could forgive it, or He could collect it. Now it was my mother's choice. She can either ask for forgiveness and repent of her sin or pay the Master His due. It is His debt to collect, not mine.

As for my mother, fifteen years after I forgave her, God asked me to sell all I had and go take care of my mother. I told God, "Surely there is someone more qualified to do this than me!" God did not answer. But that didn't keep me from complaining all the way to Ohio. God spoke to me, as I got to a sign saying "Welcome to the Buckeye State," God finally spoke to me in a disappointing tone: "Rose, Rose, Rose, when are you ever going to trust what I have done in you for her? Just trust what I have done in you for her." On the road to her house, I prayed the whole way, "God, please don't let me hurt her."

It took three more hours to get to her house because

of the snowstorm. I pulled into the driveway, and this crumpled-up old lady came out the back door. I thought, *what am I afraid of? I could knock her over with a feather!* Just then, God said, "It was necessary for you to come here and see her through your *adult eye.* You have been seeing her all these years through your *child's eye* and living in fear because of that."

I got out of the car and began to collect my things from the car (after all, I moved here!). We got in the house, and we sat at the dining room table. I looked at her across the table and said, "I'm not here because I need a mother. That is not and never has been a relationship that we have ever had, but we can be *friends.*" She looked at me, almost relieved, and said, "That sounds good."

For the next two years, I worked full time, took care of her needs by cooking, and went to the gym every other night to work out. All was going well until she fell.

Now she became almost totally dependent on me. I got a bedside commode, bathed her in a child's size blow-up swimming pool in the kitchen, washed her sheets, continued cooking for her—all while working full-time at a job. One Saturday, I came down and smelled a bad smell. She had messed herself. I came close to her and said, "Okay, it smells like bath time," as I smiled gently. I took the corner of her covers up, and she grabbed them back down. I told her, "Don't even think I am going to let you lay in this. I am a former nurse, and I know what lying in that will do to your skin." I began pulling the covers back, and her hand came up to smack me in the face. I caught it just that quick and pinned both her arms down to the bed. The fear came across her face, touching my heart. I began speaking, "I know you think that because you hurt me when I was totally dependent on you that I am going to do payback. But God sent me here to take care of you if you will let me! If you don't want me here to help you, just say, 'Rose, *get out!*' I will pack my bags and leave. I won't even look back!"

She began crying, and through her tears, she said, "How can you ever forgive me for what I did to you back then?" I told her, "You know, for years, I couldn't. But God helped me through it, and I forgave you. Don't you remember my call? I forgave you in the name of Jesus, and I have not changed my mind. Neither has God. He loves you and wants you to be happy."

Through her tears, she asked, "How can I know a God like that?" I told her, "He is my closest friend, and I can introduce you!"

I led my mom to the Lord that day, and that changed *everything*! About a week later, she confided in me that her father had passed her around sexually to her brothers to "teach them how to be a man before they get married." I began looking into "acceptable behaviors" in Serbia, where my mother's parents were born. Back there, if you could not afford housing, food, etc., you gave your daughters to the powers that be to pay for these necessities. When they got to America, those customs evolved into the type of abuse she suffered.

She has since passed away, and I sit with the joy in my heart that my mother is in heaven, in the arms of Jesus right now because I forgave her and led her to salvation. The blood of Jesus has covered all her sins.

Section Four

VISION TWO- RELATIONSHIPS, HOW TO HAVE ONE

It is funny...I have looked my whole life for someone to give me a "how-to" book on relationships. This is my lifelong research, with a revelation from God attached to it. Here goes...

A person with holes has to be careful who they select for a long-term relationship. You know that old saying? Opposites attract. Well, guess what, it is true.

Diagram 2

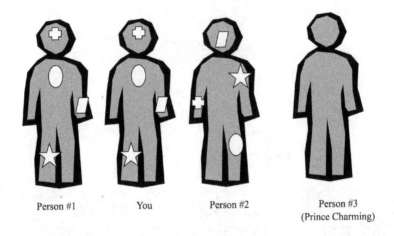

Person #1   You   Person #2   Person #3
                                                (Prince Charming)

We, as people, fall into two categories. Person #3 is not included in this count, as he is fictional.

Person #1: The person whom you see as just like you. They know where you are coming from, they think just like you, and can truly understand and feel your pain without you saying a single word. Has that ever happened to you?

Person #2: This person is, for all intent and purposes, your opposite. They have not walked in your shoes or led the kind of life you have led. You tell them about yourself, and they can empathize, but they do not fully understand where you are coming from.

Person #3: In my research, I have yet to meet Person #3, who has no holes. That would be the perfect partner.

I think Person #3 is named "Prince Charming." He is a myth. He does not exist. But we are fed our whole lives that he is real and we will live happily ever after. But the fairy tale does not ever show you what "happily ever after" looks like. You would have to figure that out on your own.

For a person with holes in their soul, the best way to help you see how to choose a person for a deep, meaningful relationship is to look at Diagram 2.

What I have come to learn through this vision I had is that the reason the You figure and Person #1 connect so well is because the You figure has the same gaping wounds they have. They can identify with the You figure because Person #1 feels the same as the You figure. They have the same holes and can tell you how painful they are.

But Person #2 is completely different. They may have as many holes in their soul as the You figure, but they are different. Their holes may even be just as bad as yours, but they are different. They can understand the You figure's "holes," but they did not go through the same life experiences as you.

When you lay Person #1 over top of the You figure, they are the same, and you can see right through the holes. Actually, everyone around you can see right through the holes in your soul as well.

But if you lay the You figure over top of Person #2,

the holes disappear. And you won't see the holes in their souls. That is because together, you cover one another's shortcomings, and together, you are made whole.

While it is wonderful to have people "understand" where you are coming from and what you have been through, it is also wonderful to be in a relationship that makes you whole. Not only that, but you also make the other person whole. That person can take a lifetime to understand and cover your holes in the soul, and you can do the same. The love will grow as you cover one another. "Carry yea one another's burdens…"

But Person #1 can't cover anything. Maybe through therapy, the You person can close holes, but it will definitely be a relationship that will require a *lot* of work.

I also think this may be the reason a lot of marriages break up. The You figure is happy with Person #2 but is strongly attracted to Person #1 because they feel that person would better understand them. That is where the myth comes in—the 80/20 rule.

While Person #2 is 80% what *you* want, there is still the 20% found in Person #1 that attracts you. Many leave the 80% for the 20%, thinking that will satisfy them, but what they get instead is to feel the holes together with their new partner. The relationship may not last long because no one wants to feel those empty holes forever.

Before, when you were with Person #2, you felt

"covered," and now with Person #1 you both feel "hollow and in pain."

FAMILY

Is it safe to assume that if many things are "off," everything is "off"?

I have five siblings which I shall use fake names for. Lance is my brother, and the rest of my siblings are women. I will call them Brenda, Betty, Audry (then me), and finally Vivian. My mother forced my brother into the mix as an abuser to do what her brothers did. Most of my sisters and I were his victims. Lance has apologized for that a few times over.

Vivian was my baby sister. We grew up very close only because we both slept in a bed in the basement because there were no bedrooms left. But when my mother threw me out of the house at the age of seventeen/eighteen, I was not permitted to see her.

Forty years later, Brenda called me out of the blue, and after about a year, she told me Vivian was living with her. Vivian, however, did not want anything to do with me. After talking to Brenda for two years, she finally told Vivian that it was safe to talk to me.

Brenda and I were together for only a few years in a group called "Witness Lee and the Local Churches," and I walked on eggshells the whole time I knew her. When I moved to Florida, God let me know that His family was my family. Perfect strangers I have met in the church now became my family. Not because I asked them to, but because God's family operates that way—with unconditional love. And that is what I needed.

Betty and I were never really close, although I did bring her to the Lord when we buried our father. She even asked if I would come to her memorial service when the time comes and tell everyone that she is going to heaven. She follows the Lord and does so much service in His name that I doubt they will need me there to say she was following the Lord.

As for Audry, I have had no contact with her, and that is her choice. We had one difference of opinion, and bam, that was it! I reached out to her a couple of times with no result.

After talking to Vivian on the phone two hours a day for two years, she asked me to move out to New Mexico with her and her husband. After a year of thinking about it, I moved out to New Mexico with her and her husband. I realize moving out there was a huge commitment on their part, and not everyone is willing or able to handle doing that much for another person. I was not sure I wanted to move from Florida to New Mexico just to be with my sister, but I did it anyway. I just wanted to be close with her and keep her close to my heart. But we got along like two peas in a pod.

I told her, "You have no idea how much I love you! You and Jim are family. Now and always." I wish every day of my life that she and I could still have a relationship. You will not always agree with my life, and I may not always agree with yours, but we are family. You don't throw family away! Vivian and I were close when we were younger because we shared a room in the basement. We got into a lot of trouble together but had fun. When I was thrown out of the house, my mother would not let me have any contact with her.

Even though I have limited relationships with my siblings, God's family is still there. They still love me, care for me, and I don't have to apologize for who and what I am.

For the most part, my birth family and I grew up like a family of strangers. Mom kept it that way so that no one would learn of all the abuse that took place in our family. I feel bad that even though Mom has passed, the legacy of hate still spreads so far into our lives that we don't even know how to love each other. We don't even know what love is.

God asks us to love one another, that is what will be required to enter heaven. To love as He loves. And who did He love? Sinners: tax collectors, prostitutes, murderers, rapists, adulterers, crazies. Jesus died for everyone's sins, whether they accept Him or not. But to get to heaven, you simply have to ask Him into your heart. Sin doesn't keep you out of heaven because God already dealt with that. What will keep you out of heaven is unbelief. Unbelief in God's Son, Jesus Christ, and what He did on the cross.

VISION #3

God gave me a vision not too long ago. I will try to
express it to you here:

Prayer of Saint Francis of Assisi

Lord, make me a channel of Thy peace;
that where there is hatred, I may bring love;
that where there is wrong, I may bring the spirit of
forgiveness;
that where there is discord, I may bring harmony;
that where there is error, I may bring truth;
that where there is doubt, I may bring faith;
that where there is despair, I may bring hope;
that where there are shadows, I may bring light;
that where there is sadness, I may bring joy.
Lord, grant that I may seek rather to comfort than to be
comforted;
to understand, than to be understood;
to love, than to be loved.

For it is by self-forgetting that one finds.
It is by forgiving that one is forgiven.
It is by dying that one awakens to eternal life.
Amen.

I lay in my bed, silent, trying to talk to God. This prayer came to my mind: "Lord, make me an instrument of Thy peace." I stopped and thought, *that doesn't* sound *right*. I got out of bed and went to google the prayer. It actually read, "Lord, make me a *channel* of Thy peace," not "instrument." I laid back down and began this discussion in my head: "Instrument, channel, what's the difference?" God began showing me. I actually shared this in an AA meeting.

I held up an ink pen (as God had shown me). I told everyone, "This is an instrument. I can use it for writing and maybe poking a hole through paper, but that is about it. An instrument has a very defined use. I can't use it, say, to pound a nail into the wall. That requires a *different* instrument. But this prayer is asking the Lord to make me a channel."

Now, what is a channel? I had to get out of bed and look that up. It is a passageway from one body of water to another, like a canal or a straw. When we become a channel, we are merely *allowing* what is in the first reservoir to pass through the channel (us) to someone else's reservoir without actually "possessing" what is going through the channel. That way, when we allow the Holy Spirit to pass through our spirit to another person, we give them *pure gold* (God).

As seen in the prayer of St. Francis of Assissi

	Left Side		Right Side
that where there is	hatred,	I may bring	love;
that where there is	wrong,	I may bring the	spirit of forgiveness;
that where there is	discord,	I may bring	harmony;
that where there is	error,	I may bring	truth;
that where there is	doubt,	I may bring	faith;
that where there is	despair,	I may bring	hope;
that where there is	shadows,	I may bring	light;
that where there is	sadness,	I may bring	joy.

If you look at that prayer again: I realized that I have no problem performing the actions on the left side of the prayer. I know how to hate, do people wrong, create discord, error, doubt, despair, bring on the shadows, and release my sadness. Those things come natural to human beings. I always want to *be* understood, and I always want to *be* loved. But I didn't for most of my life possess the ability to do that. Those are characteristics of the Holy Spirit.

What I am not so fluent doing is the words on the right side of the prayer: love, forgiveness, harmony, truth, faith, hope, light, joy, comfort. I don't usually want to be the one who understands or be the one who is doing the loving. I don't always have those qualities to give. But God does. That is why we need to give people what is on the right side of the prayer, and if we don't possess it, we can be the channel that brings the quality to them until we have that quality ourselves.

But God does possess all of those qualities! That is why we are asked to be a channel. That allows us to give what we don't possess. We merely allow God to use us as a channel for His virtues to flow through us and meet the needs of that person.

And mark my words: on that day, there will be no excuses like, "I just didn't have that particular quality to *give!*" Because a channel gives out what we do not possess.

I am changing my life. I am not always full of faith, but when I run out, I know *where* to go to get it. I have to go back to the source. God.

Anyway, just wanted to share that with you. We can *choose* to live a right life. We can choose to live on the right side of the prayer in God's presence, or live in the natural man on the left side in darkness.

As God was giving me this vision, with regard to hatred and love, I was well aware that I had holes in my soul. But what I didn't realize was how much it would skew my definition of the words in this prayer. I had no idea what love was, so how could I be expected to bring it to the table? I knew what hatred was but didn't understand the true meaning of hatred as shown in the Bible. I didn't know that hatred could stir things up like conflict or spread such bad things as shown in Galatians 5:20. This verse shows that not only is hatred an "action" word, but birds of a feather flock together, meaning hatred brings other greater actions into my life, like witchcraft, discord, jealousy, fits of rage, selfish ambition, dissensions, and factions. Sin never remains the same "size," it grows! As I hated on my mother, I can testify to the fact that I had "fits of rage" and created "discord" everywhere I went. I thought hatred was just a feeling, and I certainly did not know it had the power to do thing in my soul. I learned this by walking with God as I did my 12-step work (see below).

"That where there is hatred, I may bring love."

Hatred

Dictionary definition:
extreme dislike or disgust.

Bible definition:

Proverbs 10:12: *"Hatred stirs up conflict, but love covers over all wrongs."*

Proverbs 10:18: *"Whoever conceals hatred with lying lips and spreads slander is a fool."*

Galatians 5:20: *"Idolatry and witchcraft; hatred, discord, jealousy, fits of rage, selfish ambition, dissensions, factions."*

Love

Dictionary definition:

strong affection for another.

Bible definition:

First John 3:11: *"For this is the message you heard from the beginning: We should love one another."*

First Corinthians 13:1–3: *If I speak in the tongues of men or of angels, but do not have love, I am only a resounding gong or a clanging cymbal. If I have the gift of prophecy and can fathom all mysteries and all knowledge, and if I have a faith that can move mountains, but do not have love, I am nothing. If I give all I possess to the poor and give over my body to hardship that I may boast, but do not have love, I gain nothing.*

Matthew 5:43: *"You have heard that it was said, 'Love your neighbor and hate your enemy.'"*

Matthew 5:44: *"But I tell you, love your enemies and pray for those who persecute you."*

Matthew 5:46: *"If you love those who love you, what reward will you get? Are not even the tax collectors doing that?"*

Mark 12:30: *"Love the Lord your God with all your heart and with all your soul and with all your mind and with all your strength."*

Mark 12:33: *"To love him with all your heart, with all your understanding and with all your strength, and to love your neighbor as yourself is more important than all burnt offerings and sacrifices."*

Luke 6:27 (love for enemies): *"But to you who are listening I say: Love your enemies, do good to those who hate you."*

With regard to wrong and forgiveness, throughout my past, I did not see a relationship between these two words till I began looking them up. I saw nothing wrong with my actions against my mother; after all, all this was done *to* me, not *by* me. But if you look at the Bible regarding forgiveness, it was asking me to do something I wasn't even capable of doing, which was *forgive*. It spoke about wrong in a new way. A higher way. It spoke about it in a way in that I knew I could not even perform under my own power for my mother. It would take a higher power. That meant I would have to ask God for something I did not have, which was forgiveness for my mother.

"That where there is wrong, I may bring the spirit of forgiveness."

Wrong

Dictionary definition:

something wrong; immoral, or unethical; not according to truth or facts.

Bible definition:

First Thessalonians 5:15–19: *"Make sure that nobody pays back wrong for wrong, but always strive to do what is good for each other and for everyone else. Rejoice always, pray continually, [...]."*

Romans 13:3: *"For rulers hold no terror for those who do right, but for those who do wrong. Do you want to be free from fear of the one in authority? Then do what is right and you will be commended."*

First Corinthians 6:8: *"Instead, you yourselves cheat and do wrong, and you do this to your brothers and sisters."*

First Corinthians 6:9: *"Or do you not know that wrongdoers will not inherit the kingdom of God? Do not be deceived: Neither the sexually immoral nor idolaters nor adulterers nor men who have sex with men."*

First Corinthians 13:4–6: *"Love is patient, love is kind. It does not envy, it does not boast, it is not proud. It does not dishonor others, it is not self-seeking, it is not easily angered, it keeps no record of wrongs. Love does not delight in evil but rejoices with the truth."*

Colossians 3:25: *"Anyone who does wrong will be repaid for their wrongs, and there is no favoritism."*

James 4:3: *"When you ask, you do not receive, because you ask with wrong motives, that you may spend what you get on your pleasures."*

Forgiveness

Dictionary definition:

absolution, amnesty, pardon, remission, remittal.

Bible definition:

Matthew 26:28: *"This is my blood of the covenant, which is poured out for many for the forgiveness of sins."*

Luke 1:77: *"To give his people the knowledge of salvation through the forgiveness of their sins."*

Acts 2:38: *"Peter replied, 'Repent and be baptized, every one of you, in the name of Jesus Christ for the forgiveness of your sins. And you will receive the gift of the Holy Spirit.'"*

Acts 10:43: *"All the prophets testify about him that everyone who believes in him receives forgiveness of sins through his name."*

Acts 26:18: *"To open their eyes and turn them from darkness to light, and from the power of Satan to God, so that they may receive forgiveness of sins and a place among those who are sanctified by faith in me."*

Ephesians 1:7: *"In him we have redemption through his blood, the forgiveness of sins, in accordance with the riches of God's grace."*

Hebrews 9:22: *"In fact, the law requires that nearly everything be cleansed with blood, and without the shedding of blood there is no forgiveness."*

Discord sounds relatively harmless in the dictionary. It sounds like a minor thing. But if you look at what the Bible says below, it groups "discord" with things that are really very serious, such as "witchcraft or slander or fits of rage." When the Lord was taking me through the process of forgiveness for my mother, I experienced extreme fits of rage. I could not even control it. That was one of my holes in my soul crying out in pain. But God, by healing my wounds, brought me into harmony with Him and his people.

"That where there is discord, I may bring harmony."

Discord

Dictionary definition:

lack of agreement or harmony (as between persons, things, or ideas).

Bible definition:

Second Corinthians 12:20: *"For I am afraid that when I come I may not find you as I want you to be, and you may not find me as you want me to be. I fear that there may be discord, jealousy, fits of rage, selfish ambition, slander, gossip, arrogance and disorder."*

Galatians 5:20: *"Idolatry and witchcraft; hatred, discord, jealousy, fits of rage, selfish ambition, dissensions, factions."*

Harmony

Dictionary definition:

the combination of simultaneous musical notes in a chord.

Bible definition:

Romans 12:16: *"Live in* **harmony** *with one another. Do not be proud, but be willing to associate with people of low position. Do not be conceited."*

Second Corinthians 6:15: *What* **harmony** *is there between Christ and Belial? Or what does a believer have in common with an unbeliever?"*

I was not even aware that I was acting in error until I found these scriptures in the Word. The Scriptures really are the power of God. The word "error" sounds like a minor mistake, as it says you are ignorant of a code of behavior. That doesn't sound too bad, does it? But the Word of God is the code of behavior, and the only way you would know that is if you turn from the error in your life to God, and He saves you from a multitude of sins. You see, when you are in a state of error, your sins multiply. You have to make your way to truth. Truth is more than what the dictionary says it is. The Bible says truth has the power to set you free. This book has done that for me. Letting out all the "secrets" of my past has given me a freedom I could have only have imagined. Only Jesus can free us like that. He is truth. Truth then becomes a path to God the Father.

"That where there is error, I may bring truth."

Error

Dictionary definition:
> an act or condition of ignorant or imprudent deviation from a code of behavior.

Bible definition:
> Matthew 22:29: *"Jesus replied, 'You are in error because you do not know the Scriptures or the power of God.'"*

James 5:20: *"Remember this: Whoever turns a sinner from the error of their way will save them from death and cover over a multitude of sins."*

Truth

Dictionary definition:

sincerity in action, character, and utterance.

Bible definition:

John 8:32: *"Then you will know the truth, and the truth will set you free."*

John 1:14: *"The glory of the one and only Son, who came from the Father, full of grace and truth."*

John 14:6: *"Jesus answered, 'I am the way and the truth and the life. No one comes to the Father except through me.'"*

When you experience having a rug of life ripped out from underneath you growing up by having parents who acted contrary to the values of society, it causes you to doubt everything in your life. That doubt carried on till I had walked with the Lord for several years, and I didn't even know it. But when Jesus began introducing me to a life of faith, my doubting stood out like a sore thumb. When you read in the Word what faith can do, such as forming an entire universe out of nothing or moving a mountain, and how God says without faith it is impossible to please Him, it became something I strove for.

"That where there is doubt, I may bring faith."

Doubt

Dictionary definition:
> to call into question the truth of; to be uncertain or in doubt about.

Bible definition:

> Matthew 14:31: *" 'You of little faith,' he said, 'why did you doubt?'"*

> Mark 11:23: *"Truly I tell you, if anyone says to this mountain, 'Go, throw yourself into the sea,' and does not doubt in their heart but believes that what they say will happen, it will be done for them."*

> James 1:6: *"But when you ask, you must believe and not doubt, because the one who doubts is like a wave of the sea, blown and tossed by the wind."*

Faith

Dictionary definition:

> belief and trust in and loyalty to God; belief in
> the traditional doctrines of a religion; firm belief
> in something for which there is no proof.

Bible definition:

> Hebrews 11:1–3: *"Now faith is confidence*
> *in what we hope for and assurance about*
> *what we do not see. This is what the ancients*
> *were commended for. By faith we understand*
> *that the universe was formed at God's*
> *command, so that what is seen was not made*
> *out of what was visible."*

> Hebrews 11:6: *"And without faith it is*
> *impossible to please God, because anyone*
> *who comes to him must believe that he exists*
> *and that he rewards those who earnestly*
> *seek him."*

> Matthew 9:29: *"According to your faith let*
> *it be done to you."*

I have to say, out of all of the words in the prayer of St.
Francis of Assisi, the one that stood out to me the most was
"despair." I felt utterly hopeless and totally lost in my life.
I felt crushed and inadequate by my despair. This caused
me to work harder on the job than anyone else because
I felt inferior to them. Then I worked for a man on a job
who added "value" to me. He gave me a performance

appraisal of 115% out of 120%. I remember quizzing him on why didn't I get 120% and what I could have done better. He stated that he *must* give me something to strive for and that 115% was really good. He stated that a lot of the people around the company only got 60%. It took him saying that for me to realize I had value. As I taped that appraisal to my refrigerator, it gave me hope. No one could then tell me I was worthless because this one person gave me value. Then Jesus began showing me that he valued me as well and would never put me to shame.

"That where there is despair, I may bring hope."

Despair

Dictionary definition:
> utter loss of hope.

Bible definition:

> Second Corinthians 4:8: *"We are hard pressed on every side, but not crushed; perplexed, but not in despair."*

Hope

Dictionary definition:
> to want something to happen or be true.

Bible definition:

> Romans 5:3–5: *"Not only so, but we also glory in our sufferings, because we know that suffering produces perseverance;*

perseverance, character; and character, hope. And hope does not put us to shame, because God's love has been poured out into our hearts through the Holy Spirit, who has been given to us."

Romans 8:24: *"For in this hope we were saved. But hope that is seen is no hope at all. Who hopes for what they already have?"*

Have you ever been writing, and someone walks behind you, and the only reason you know they are there is because they are blocking the light? That is how it was when I began realizing that something was missing in my life. The only reason you can be blinded by darkness is you go from a well-lit room to total darkness. Then you are blinded for a period of time till your eyes adjust to the dark. The Word below tells you that you walk around in darkness blind. But there is one place that you don't experience that, and it is in the shadow of the Almighty. God sees everything! We can't even hide in the darkness because the light and dark are the same to Him. Growing up, I always hated the dark!

"That where there are shadows, I may bring light."

Shadows

Dictionary definition:

> partial darkness or obscurity within a part of space from which rays from a source of light are cut off by an interposed opaque body.

Bible definition:

> First John 2:11: *"But anyone who hates a brother or sister is in the darkness and walks around in the darkness. They do not know where they are going, because the darkness has blinded them."*

> Psalm 91:1: *"Whoever dwells in the shelter of the Most High will rest in the shadow of the Almighty."*

Light

Internet article:

> I read on the internet that there are approximately 107 forms of light operating at all times, and most of these operate in total darkness.

Bible definition:

> Psalm 139:11–12: *"If I say, 'Surely the darkness will hide me and the light become night around me,' even the darkness will not be dark to you; the night will shine like the day, for darkness is as light to you."*

John 8:12: *"When Jesus spoke again to the people, he said, 'I am the light of the world. Whoever follows me will never walk in darkness, but will have the light of life.'"*

John 3:21: *"But whoever lives by the truth comes into the light, so that it may be seen plainly that what they have done has been done in the sight of God."*

First John 1:5: *"This is the message we have heard from him and declare to you: God is light; in him there is no darkness at all."*

Sadness was my constant companion, and yes, growing up, fear was also my constant companion. I would have given anything for the joy I saw in my friends' lives. The moment Jesus entered my life, I experienced joy for the first time, along with all of joy's "friends." Like I have said before, birds of a feather flock together. Salvation changed my life!

"That where there is sadness, I may bring joy."

Sadness

Dictionary definition:
  expressing of grief or unhappiness.

Bible definition:

Nehemiah 2:2: *"So the king asked me, 'Why does your face look so sad when you are not ill? This can be nothing but sadness of heart.' I was very much afraid."*

Joy

Dictionary definition:

> emotion evoked by well-being, success, or good fortune or by the prospect of possessing what one desires.

Bible definition:

> *Galatians 5:22: "But the fruit of the Spirit is love, joy, peace, forbearance, kindness, goodness, faithfulness."*

Jesus can change your life! He can change your path and direction. As my holes got filled, my direction changed, and so did my life. He can do that to you too.

IMAGINE—A SOUL WITH NO HOLES!

I was on my way to my twelve-step program, all ready to say those words, you know, the words, "Hi, I'm _____, and I am an alcoholic." I was halfway to the meeting when that small voice in my soul said, "I don't like you calling yourself something you are not. I delivered you from that." I stopped and thought for a moment. *That's right; God is the Great Physician. He never heals people halfway. He heals people for a purpose! And He heals them all the way.* Complete healing! *How do I know that? Because I know my God!*

I began to get excited. I am fully recovered from alcoholism. I don't want to drink anymore, but for a totally different reason. I don't want to risk the relationship I have with my God. I have a hope and a future now. But that didn't happen overnight. It took years of walking with God, reading His Word, and doing what He said to do.

91

I know…a lot of people will say, "Well, I just don't hear God. He doesn't talk to me." Then why does the Bible say, "My sheep hear my voice, and they follow Me"? I began doing research on that and came up with a clue. *If you want to hear and listen to His voice today, you need to start by reading and listening to what He has already said in the past.* That means reading His Word and praying a verse now and then back to Him in the form of a prayer. That lets God know you are interested in what He has already said and that you want more! So, I did just that. I looked through the Bible and said, "God, where do I start?" I came to the book of Hebrews. Before alcohol got the best of me, I read Hebrews continually for years.

I began reading one chapter a night. Then I picked a verse (any verse) and began using the words of that verse as I prayed. I learned a long time ago that my prayers don't have to be long-winded and fancy, but if I just pray the words in the verses I read, that is just fine. I pray a verse, thanking Him for what the verse says.

Now I know what you're thinking… "I don't understand the Bible—it is like Greek to me!"

There are two reasons why it may be like that:

1. Have you asked Jesus into your heart? Your human spirit needs to be made alive so that you can receive what the Word is giving.

2. It is okay if you read the Word and don't have

complete understanding. Why then, do you say, should I even read it? What you are reading is a spiritual language, and it was written by God for the Holy Spirit to nourish your human spirit. In other words, it is not food for your mind; it is a spiritual feast.

After reading the Bible, I would sit back, open my arms (which is body language for "I am open to receive"), and I would pray:

"Lord, I take in Your Word to let You know I want a relationship with You. Now is Your time to speak to me, if, *if*, You wish to. I am going to just listen for Your voice because I belong to You!" I sat there for ten minutes or so, and after doing this for a while, God saw that I *wanted* to listen, and I began hearing His voice.

I am in the Word numerous times throughout the week, and it is amazing to have joy that is overflowing and more peace than I thought possible.

I share my relationship with God with anyone who will listen, and the more I share, the fuller I get. But that's not all…

I remember before starting down this path feeling so empty and feeling so "less-than" and feeling like everyone was always a step ahead of me. All I could see was the problems in my own life and no way to fix them. I could see no future. I thought I was permanently broken!

But by doing these few simple things: reading His Word, praying, and listening, I noticed that these gaping holes in my life have closing and I am walking through life knowing I won't fall. My God walks *with* me! The holes in my soul are *no more*. God filled them when I wasn't looking, rather when I wasn't focused on them, but being focused on Him. I am finally on level ground and can walk without fear of falling.

But it is easy to rest on your laurels. If you do, you can fall back to your previous state. You have to be vigilant, staying in the word, remaining in His presence, and be ever so cautious not to drift away.

Remain!

Section Five

SEASONS

I remember something an old man told me. I was sitting in church, the service had ended, and he came up to me, noticing I was crying. He asked what I was crying about. I told him, "I feel like such a failure compared to everyone here." He told me a story of his past. "Our lives contain *seasons*, periods of time where God works on and with us to make us more like Him."

"When I was a farmer, every year in Spring, I had to till the fields. By doing that, I removed all the rocks so I could plant my crops." The rocks were pulled over to the side of the field. Then, he began to plant. "Soon, Summer arrived, and water and sun came causing the plants to begin to grow. In the Fall, harvesttime came, and the plants were cut down and made ready for distribution to others. Now came Winter, and the ground was laid to rest."

In Spring, it started all over again. The soil was tilled, and low and behold, more rocks were brought to the edge.

He said, "You would think that maybe the farmer didn't do such a good job the year before, but that just isn't true."

"It is like our Christian life: God does some tilling in our hearts, and rocks appear. Those rocks represent the deficiencies or sins in our life. He pulls them up so we can deal with them. You may ask, 'well, why doesn't He just pull them all up at once and get it over with?'" He said, "If God showed us everything that is wrong with us at one time, we would throw our hands up and say, '*I give up*!' But in His mercy, He shows us a little of what He wants to change and lets us come to Him and deal with it."

"And if we let God deal with these things in our life, we will see growth and soon a spiritual harvest that we can give to the world."

But He is not done with me yet. The second I think I am becoming more like Christ, He shows me something else...

50TH YEAR HIGH SCHOOL REUNION

I only remember all the kids at school tormenting me, making fun of me, and getting me into trouble every chance they got. But I was too busy trying to survive childhood to even care. I had *no* friends and was liked by no one. Every five years, my mother told me that people contacted her and told her the reunion was happening, but my response was always, "So what!" Now that my mother has passed on and the family home was sold, they got a hold of me through social media. I made a decision to go but decided to bring a friend so that way I would have someone to talk to while everyone ignored me.

I complained about it the whole drive there (19 hours away). My friend encouraged me to go because his experience going to his 50th was so wonderful. Yuck!

We checked into our hotel and got ready for the event.

It was right down the road from our hotel. We walked in, checked in with the welcome table, and received a gift with our name tags. We went into a large ballroom, and tables were decorated gayly, and people were seated all over. I picked a table closest to the door (for a quick get-a-way), and we sat down. As our table began to fill up, one of the ladies began to introduce herself. I cringed because she was one of my biggest "haters" back in the day. When I told her my name, she said, "Oh, you were the quiet one. I remember your sister; she was involved in everything!" I said, "Yeah, she was a social chameleon while I was busy surviving childhood." She asked what I meant, and I told her some of the highlights of my childhood. She said, "Oh, I'm sorry—we never knew." I told her, "No one did." (Actually, we were not allowed to have friends or do things at school other than learning. We had half an hour to get home, or we got beat.)

I tried to make small talk with her by asking her what she had been up to since high school. She told me that she was on the mission field a couple of times. My heart skipped a beat! My tormentor is a missionary? I couldn't believe it. The man sitting next to her, who was a football player, said how he is now a pastor. He said that at another reunion, another classmate said the same thing happened to her, as happened to me.

Now my mind began to spin. Someone else went through what I went through? Several other classmates were also pastors, and a lot of lives had been transformed. I couldn't believe my eyes.

One of my classmates had hung onto my yearbook for fifty years! She handed it to me and said how glad she was that I was there. I decided to let people sign it. I handed it to fellow students and asked them to sign, and they did. I could not help thinking that if I had gotten that yearbook fifty years ago, would anyone have signed it?

As I sat there looking around, I began talking to the Lord in my heart. *You have been working in my life for these last fifty years, why did I think you wouldn't work in their lives as well?* Then, I got sad that I had not gone to more reunions over the years. I noted that everyone in this class seemed to be very close, and I probably really missed out!

PARADIGM SHIFT

This represents what I have discovered. What is a paradigm shift? The dictionary says it is an important change that happens when the usual way of thinking about or doing something is replaced by a new and different way. This discovery will bring about a paradigm shift in our understanding of the changes being made in our life.

I saw people who were so different than what I remember them to be. It was a miracle! I was so caught up in my own life that I did not even consider that God would work in their lives as well. God is not willing that *any* should perish but that all would come to know Him. I spent a lot of years hating on these people when God spent a lot of time loving on them. Years ago, when I accepted Jesus as my Savior, He told me that His family was now *my* family.

Going from a rough childhood, finding Jesus a week before my 18th birthday, marrying an abusive man, having two children, and seeing all the changes God has made in my life to present, I would say He has shifted my paradigm permanently.

All a paradigm shift requires is a shift in your perspective. God has shifted mine yet again, and it means He is not done with me yet. There is more in my life that God needs to change, and *I am willing*!

FINAL THOUGHTS

I have never thought of myself as a writer. It has never been my intention to do this for a living. Writing this book was due to a couple of visions from God, and after recording the visions, God instructed me to do my autobiography in the hopes that it would reach others who have gone down the path of abuse as a child. I have helped a lot of people of all ages struggling with the same issues as I did, and I am grateful that God has used me like that to help them.

If you find this book helps you as well, send me an email at PMROSE2020@AOL.COM. Put "REGARDING YOUR BOOK" in the subject line. I will respond, I promise.